Claudia Stein

Tel Aviv 2019
The Culture Guide

© 2018 Claudia Stein (text, maps, photos)

ISBN 9781728785073

Imprint: privately published

Table Of Contents

Preface

Israel's secular hot-spot hosts an abundant amount of museums, art galleries, and other cultural venues and is home to country's only opera house. This guide will help you discover the local scene even without speaking a word of Hebrew. The summary of the city's history gives you the eyes of a local and the tips on cafés and restaurants make sure you can fully concentrate on enjoying the richness of the dynamic cultural life while correctly being taken care of.

Tel Aviv, October 2018

Claudia Stein

http://www.stein-books.com

instagram: @steinbooks

PS.

Please note: this book is an extract of the comprehensive travel guide by the same author.

Museums

Tel Aviv offers a much-diversified range of museums and the local art scene, in particular, plays in the same league as those in big cosmopolitan cities. Even though these treasures are hidden behind unimpressive walls, the visitor soon will notice: Tel Aviv is shaking, and something is moving! The museums of the neighboring cities bring the offer down to a round figure. This guide only lists the highlights in these other cities, not all the venues. They are only 5-10 km away from the center of Tel Aviv and can be reached by bus or taxi.

!!! The public and religious museums close on Friday in the early afternoon until Sunday. Museums that are open on Saturday normally close on Sunday.

In this book, the museums are subdivided into the following categories:

- **City History**
- History of Tel Aviv Museum
- Shalom-Tower
- **Pre-State-History**
- Independence Hall
- ETZEL-Museum
- HAGANA-Museum
- LEHI-Museum
- IDF-Museum
- Jabotinsky Institute
- Palmach-Museum
- **Biographies**
- Ben-Gurion House

- Bialik Museum
- **Art Museums**
- Tel Aviv Museum of Art
- Helena Rubinstein Pavilion for Contemporary Art
- Ilana Goor Museum
- Nachum Gutman Museum
- Rokach Haus
- Rubin Museum
- **Religious Museums**
- Beit Hatefutsot (House of the Diaspora)
- **Israeli History and Culture**
- Eretz-Israel-Museum
- Israel-Museum
- **Museum in Ramat Gan**
- Harry Oppenheimer Diamond Museum
- **Museums in Holon**
- Museum for Digital Art
- Children's Museum
- Cartoon Museum
- Design Museum

City History

1.) The first city hall of Tel Aviv is now home to the new museum for urban history, the **Beit HaIr, History of Tel Aviv Museum**, inaugurated in 2009 for the city's 100th birthday. In preparation for Tel Aviv's 100th birthday celebration in 2009, many unique exhibits were collected that were reminiscent of the era before the proclamation of the state. The result is an extraordinary exhibition with old photo collections, films and the office of the first mayor, Meir Dizengoff, and interactive computer installations. 27, Bialik St., Tel. 03-724.0311, Mo.–Th. 09.00–17.00, Fr.–Sa. + holidays 10.00–14.00, Su. closed. http://www.beithair.org

2.) There is hardly another building that has raised as much public dispute as the **Shalom Tower** (migdal shalom) Until 1958, the first Hebrew-speaking high school in the world – the Herzliya Gymnasium – was located here and the demolition of the historic building has been regretted many times ever since. When the Shalom Tower was inaugurated in 1965, it was Israel's highest building with 39 floors. The photo exhibition in the hall and on the first floor is well worth seeing, even though the texts are mainly in Hebrew, as are the famous mosaic works on the walls that tell the history of the city. 9, Achad Ha'am, Tel. 03-510.0337, Su.-Th. 08.00-19.00, Fr. 08.00-14.00. http://www.migdalshalom.co.il.

Pre-State-History

The historic museums in Israel are rather "political museums"; the country is young (founded in 1948) and its history is inseparably connected to the political events in the Near East. Politics are part of everyday life and if you want to understand Israel, then you might be interested in spending about an hour in the **ETZEL museum** at the Charles Clore Park (close to the beach)

9

where the events of 1947/48 are explicitly explained. The visitor will learn about the background of what still dominates the news today.

3.) **Independence Hall** is the name of the house where Israeli history was made. In this building, David Ben-Gurion proclaimed the State Israel on 5 Iyar 5708 (14 May 1948) only a couple of hours before the British left the country. The museum preserved everything exactly as it was: the same furniture and the same name tags on the reserved seats and many other exhibits that document the birth of the new state. Rothschild 16, Tel. 03-517.3942, Su.-Th. 09.00-17.00, Fr. 09.00-14.00. http://ihi.org.il

The Israeli Defense Forces (IDF) are in charge of 5 historic museums, of which 4 deal with the Jewish resistance groups ETZEL (also called "Irgun"), LEHI and HAGANA. The museums are: IDF History Museum, ETZEL Museum, LEHI Museum, HAGANA Museum and another extra ETZEL Museum that only deals with the War of Independence 1947/48 (at Charles Clore Park.) You can get a combined ticket for all those museums that is valid for one month.

!!! Make sure you bring your passport; access might be denied without it.

4.) The **ETZEL Museum** documents the activities of this resistance group who not only fought against the Arab attacks against Jews but also against the British who did not protect the Jews enough against the Arab assaults and would minimize Jewish immigration to Palestine during WWII; Jews were sent back to Europe which, for many, was a death sentence. The main goal of ETZEL was the establishment of a Jewish State within the territory of the British Mandate according to the Balfour Declaration of 1917.

The museum has two branches: a) 38, King George St. (close to Gan Meir Park and Dizengoff Square,) where the general history of the organization is exhibited, and b) at the beach on the way to Jaffa (Charles Clore Park, close to HaTachana, old train station) where only the events between 1947/48 are displayed in detail. 38, King George St., Tel. 03-528.4001, Charles Clore Park, Tel. 03-517.7180, both Su.–Th. 08.00–16.00.

5.) The HAGANA is the predecessor of the ZAHAL, the Israeli Army. The **HAGANA Museum** is located in the house of its founder Eliyahu Golomb and shows the evolution of the organization that initially had been founded for self-defense. In 1909, HaShomer (the watchman) was founded after several Arab assaults on Jews during the second Aliya between 1904 and 1914. From 1929 on, the HAGANA became the biggest and also technically best-equipped and experienced among the resistance groups. Like ETZEL, they also fought against the British and for more protection of the Palestinian Jews. During WWII, they organized the clandestine immigration of European Jews . Prominent members of the HAGANA included Yitzhak Rabin, Ariel Sharon, and Dr. Ruth Westheimer. 23, Rothschild Blvd., Tel. 03-560.8624, Su.–Th. 08.30–16.00, hagana_museum@mod.gov.il

6.) The **Lehi Museum – Beit Yair** (or House Stern) is dedicated to Avraham Yair Stern and his resistance group LEHI during the time of the British Mandate (1918-1948.) LEHI had split from ETZEL, and of all resistance groups, they were the most radical. The British had been their main enemy and to defeat them, they even considered collaborating with Nazi Germany and ultimately, also to bring the unwanted Jews from Europe to the Holy Land. 8, Stern St. , Tel. 03-682.0288, Su.–Th. 08.30–16.00; http://www.lehi.org.il

7.) The **IDF History Museum** (Israeli Defense Force) is a direct neighbor of the old train station HaTachana between Jaffa and Tel Aviv. The visit leads through 13 little halls and 6 small sites where the history of the Israeli Army is documented with military uniforms, weapons, technical developments, files, videos, and even a comprehensive tank exhibition. Tel Aviv Promenade (Tayelet), HaMered St./Yehezkel Kaufman St., Tel. 03-517.2913, Su.–Th. 08.30–15.30; toldot_zahal_museum@mod.gov.il

8.) The **Jabotinsky Institute** goes far beyond the biography of its founder Ze'ev Jabotinsky. Based on an imaginary conversation, Jabotinsky explains to his son the events happening at that time. The film "Af al pi chen" (Hebrew for Anyway) about the clandestine immigration from Europe, the so-called Aliya Bet, is well worth watching.King George St. 38, 1st floor, Tel. 03-528.6523, Su.-Th. 08.00-16.00, http://www.jabotinsky.org, office@jabotinsky.org

9.) The **Palmach Museum** is mentioned here for the sake of completeness. It is open to tourists, but a visit requires prior reservation. If you are in the area, just go by anyway, you might get lucky that day and be allowed to get an impression without having to take the tour. The tour takes 90 minutes, and audio guides can be obtained in different languages. The Palmach was the Elite division of the HAGANA and very different from all the other groups. First of all, they temporarily collaborated with the British, and all the members also lived in Kibbutzim where they worked 14 days a month as a way of life. Haim Levanon St. 10, Tel. 03- 545.9800, Su-Th, closed on Shabbat. palmach_reservation@mod.gov.il, http://info.palmach.org.il

Biographies

Some museums are dedicated to public figures like Chaim Bialik, Yitzhak Rabin or David Ben-Gurion. In most cases, the street is also named after them.

10.) The **Ben-Gurion House** is where Israel's first Prime Minister, David Ben-Gurion and his wife Paula lived. The house and all furniture and personal belongings are preserved as they were, including the comprehensive private library. The visitor gains insight of the public and private life of the politician. Ben-Gurion Boulevard 17, Tel. 03-522.1010, Su.-Th. 08.00-15.00, Mo. -17.00, Fr. 08.00-13.00, Sa. 11.00-14.00, http://www.bg-house.org, bghouse@bezeqint.net

11.) **Chaim Nachman Bialik** was one of the most celebrated among the Israeli poets and renowned for his children books. The interior of this villa from 1925 is worth the visit: a colorful mix of different styles, very typical for its time. Bialik St. 22, Tel. 03-525.4530, Mo.-Th. 09.00-17.00, Fr. + Sa. 10.00-14.00, http://www.beithair.org

Art

Tel Aviv is rich in art, whether galleries, art museums or even in the street.

12.) The **Tel Aviv Museum of Art** is the primary point of reference for the Israeli art scene. The museum is subdivided into the main house, the Helena Rubinstein Pavilion for Contemporary Art and the spectacular Herta and Paul Amir building. In addition to different collections and works of Israeli and international artists, the museum offers a wide range of activities with special exhibitions, readings, dance performances, and films. Among the collections are also the famous "Miniature Rooms" by Helena Rubinstein. The Pavilion for

Contemporary Art is not at the same address as the rest of the museum; it is a neighbor of the theater HaBima at the end of Rothschild Blvd. 27, Tel. 03-607.7000, Mo., We., Sa. 10.00-18.00, Tu. + Th. 10.00-21.00, Fr. 10.00-14.00, http://www.tamuseum.com, info@tamuseum.com.

13.) The **Helena Rubinstein Pavilion for Contemporary Art** is not only set apart from the Tel Aviv Museum of Art, but it also has an outstanding personality: it is a platform the Art Museum provides for young artists. Tarsat Blvd. 6, Tel. 03- 528.7196, Mo., We., Sa. 10.00-18.00, Tu. + Th. 10.00-21.00, Fr. 10.00-14.00, http://www.tamuseum.com

14.) The **Nachum Gutman Museum** is located in the Writer's House that used to be the seat of the newspaper "HaPoel HaZair." The museum shows many of Gutman's works which are not only a collection of extraordinary paintings; he was also famous for his prose, children's books, and illustrations. His mosaic works decorate the walls of the hall in the Shalom Tower. The museum also shows works of lesser-known names and of Arab Israelis as well who focus on the depiction of the Arab culture in Israeli art. Rokach St. 21, Tel. 03-516.1970, Mo.-Th. 10.00-16.00, Fr. 10.00-14.00, Sa. 10.00-15.00. http://www.gutmanmuseum.co.il/en

15.) The **Ilana Goor Museum** is an institution in Jaffa. The artist has spent many years in refurbishing this ruin from the 18th century for private and public use. In Ilana's atelier, no everyday item is safe from being turned into art. The museum shows paintings, sculptures, and furniture from Ilana Goor and other artists. The view from the roof terrace is breathtaking. Mazal Dagim St. 4, Tel. 03-683.7676, Su-Fr 10.00-16.00, Sa 10.00-17.00, before holidays 10.00-14.00. http://www.ilanagoormuseum.org

16.) The **Rokach House** was built in 1887 by Shimon Rokach, one of the founding fathers of Neve Tzedek. His house was one the first in the new neighborhood outside of Jaffa. The house had been saved from being torn down by Rokach's grand-daughter, the sculptor Leah Majaro-Mintz, then refurbished and finally opened for exhibitions. Even though the documentation in the museum is entirely in Hebrew, the film about the first years of Neve Tzedek can also be seen in English. The historic photo collection is also very interesting, as much as Leah's works and the furniture from the late 19th century. Rokach St. 36, Tel. 03-516.8042, Th-Sa 10.00-14.00 http://rokach-house.co.il/, info@rokach-house.co.il.

17.) The **Rubin Museum** is where artist Reuven Rubin lived and worked. from 1946 until his death in 1974. His works are an example for early Israeli art. Many of his works reflect life in the city of Tel Aviv and Palestine before the founding of the State of Israel. The museum presents a permanent exhibition — often complemented with special shows, the original atelier, a room with his private belongings and a reading room. Families and children are very welcome and can participate in the workshops. The museum exhibits online the works of children who were inspired by Reuven Rubin. Bialik St. 14, Tel. 03-525.5961, Mo., Wed., Th. + Fr. 10.00-15.00. Tu. 10.00-20.00, Sa. + holidays 11.00-14.00, So. closed. http://www.rubinmuseum.org.il

Religious Museums

18.) The **Beit Hatefutsot** (Hebrew for House of the Diaspora) is the Museum of the Jewish Diaspora. The history of the last 2,000 years of the Jews outside of Israel is told on several floors. The museum is innovative and examines the subject from different angles with additional temporary exhibitions. Tel Aviv University Campus, Klausner St.; Matatia Gate 2, Tel. 3-745.7808, Su -We 10.00-17.00, Th 10.00-22.00, Fr 09.00-14.00, Sa. 10.00-15.00, http://www.bh.org.il

Israeli History and Culture

There are two museums with a very similar name: the Eretz Israel Museum and the Israeli Museum; they are even on the same street. The first is an open-air museum, the other one belongs to the Yitzhak Rabin Center.

19.) The **Eretz Israel Museum** is located in the north of Tel Aviv close to Yarkon Park. The museum emphasizes the diversity of the Land of Israel (Eretz Israel): archeology, botany, culture, folklore, modern life, etc. Within the park-like outdoor installation, little pavilions show different aspects. The entrance fee for the planetarium is not included in the museum ticket. Haim Levanon St. 2, Tel. 03-641-5244, Mo.+ We. 10.00-16.00, Tu.+Th. 10.00-20.00, Fr. 10.00-14.00, Sa. 10.00-16.00. http://www.eretzmuseum.org.il

20.) The impressive architecture of the **Yitzhak Rabin Center** with the Israeli Museum inside is difficult to miss; the white roof resembles the Sydney Opera House from far away. This museum deals with modern Israeli society and the development of democracy. It exhibits political events in Israel during the lifetime of Yitzhak Rabin and gives an insight into the private person Yitzhak Rabin behind the prominent politician. The museum belongs to the Yitzhak Rabin Center which was inaugurated in November 2005, 10 years after Rabin was murdered. The center researches the effects the murder had on the Israeli society. Guided tours are available every hour, but reservations are recommended. Haim Levanon St. 14, Tel. 03-745.3313/ 19, Su, Mo, We 09.00-17.00, Tu.+Th 09.00-19.00, Fr 09.00-14.00, www.rabincenter.org.il

Marina

Hayarkon

Ben Yehuda

Allenby

Herbert Samuel

HaYarkon

Daniel

Shlomo Lahat Promenade

Prof. Yehezkel Kaufmann

4b

7

14

16

Eilat

Frenkel

Florentin

David Raziel

Elifelet

Marzuk Ve-Azar

HaAliyaShniya

Old Jaf a Oleo Zion

15

Dereck

Yehuda Meragusa

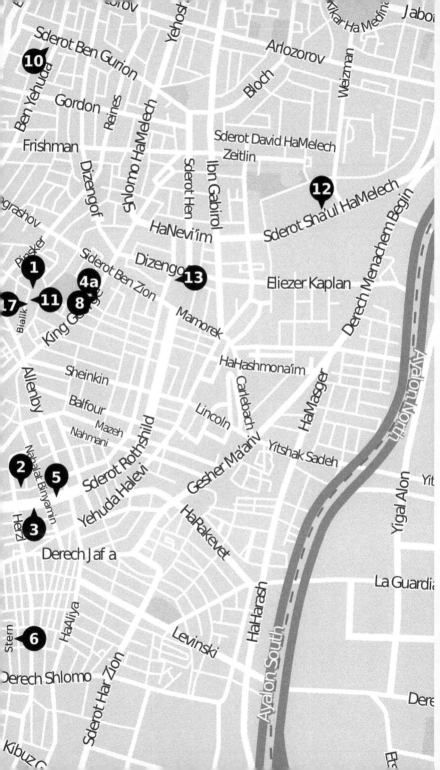

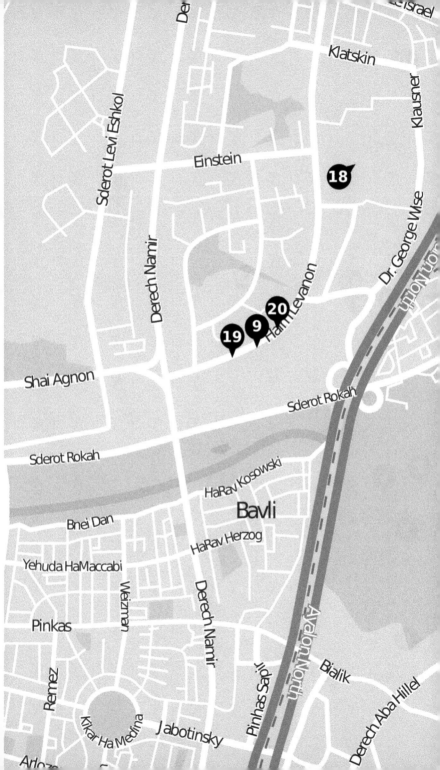

Museums in Holon

Holon is located south of Tel Aviv and very well connected by bus. From Rothschild Blvd., it is only 8 km, and even a taxi is not too expensive. Bus No. 3 leaves from Rothschild/Lilienblum. If you do not have much time, you should definitely make sure you do not miss the Design Museum (4.)

1.) The **Israeli Center for Digital Art** is an alternative museum for video, audio and digital art in general. The exhibiting artists come from all over the world, not only Israel. HaAmoraim St. 4, Holon, Tel. 03-556.8792, Tu 16.00-20.00, We-Th 14.00-18.00. Bus Nr. 3: stop Aharonovich/ HaTsionut. www.digitalartlab.org.il

2.) The **Children's Museum** is a fantastic place for children aged 2-10. A reservation is needed all events are moderated. Currently, there are activities in Hebrew and English, but you should ask about your language; the museum is might offer something that suits you. Mifrats Shlomo St. 1, Holon. Tel. 03-650.3006, Bus Nr. 3 stop „Mifrats Shlomo/ Moshe Sharet" http://www.childrensmuseum.org.il

3.) The **Cartoon Museum** is the first of its kind in Israel. The permanent exhibition is as manifold as the events with international artists that show the visitor the necessity for caricature in society. Weizman St. 61, Holon, Tel. 03-652.1849, Mo.+We. 10:00-13:00, Tu+Th., 17:00-20:00, Sa. 10:00-15:00, Bus Nr. 3: stop HaHistadrut/ Weizman, http://www.cartoon.org.il

4.) The new **Design Museum** is already impressive from the outside, but the admiration continues inside. Constantly changing exhibitions with international artists, monthly special venues and activities for the whole family (like "Nights in the Museum") turn the museum into a very special place. Pinhas Eilon St. 8, Holon, Tel.

073-215.1515, Mo.+We. 10.00-16.00, Tu. 10.00-20.00, Th. 10.00-18.00, Fr. 10.00-14.00, Sa. 11.00-20.00, Bus Nr. 3: stop Golda Meir / Holon Kanyion (Shopping Mall). http://www.dmh.org.il

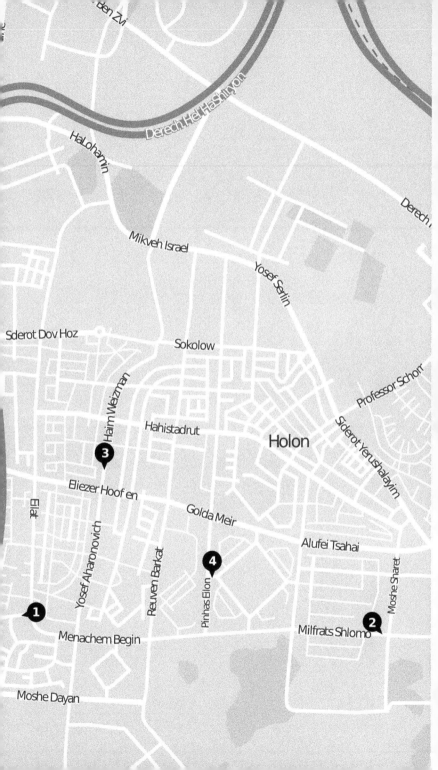

Galleries

The ethnic and cultural plurality of Israel is also reflected in the gallery scene. It is impossible to list all galleries, there are probably around 100 in Tel Aviv. This selection contains the most renowned, established, alternative, critical, etc.,... among them.

1.) The **Center for Contemporary Art (CCA)** is by far one of the most creative spaces in Tel Aviv with a huge archive for video art with currently about 3,000 works. The CCA also offers workshops for children as well as extension studies for film artists and curators. A visit to the CCA is an absolute must if you want to get acquainted with the local scene. Kalisher 5, Tel. 03-510.6111, Mo-Th. 14:00-19:00, Fr-Sa 10:00-14:00, http://cca.org.il, info@cca.org.il

2.) **Dvir** is THE reference for established Israeli and international artists and those who are about to consolidate their career. The gallery participates in international art fairs (Frieze New York, Art Basel, etc.). Thus the art exhibited in their own space is of top-class. Hizkiyahu HaMelech 1, Tel. 03-604.3003, Tu.-Th. 11.00-18.00, Fr.-Sa. 10.00-13.00, http://www.dvirgallery.com

3.) Since its founding in 1985, the **Chelouche Gallery** has exhibited works from local and international artists and is today renowned for contemporary art. The works are extensive and of diverse characters and forms: sculptures, video art, paintings, installations, etc. In October 2010, the gallery moved to Mazeh Street, a spectacular building by Josef Berliner, the so-called "Twin House." It was the first of its kind and was supposed to be the home of the architect and his brother, but later, the Association of Architects and Engineers and the Academy for Architecture moved in. Mazeh St. 7, Tel. 03-620.0068,

Mo-Th 11.00-19.00, Fr 10.00-14.00, Sa 11.00-14.00, www.chelouchegallery.com

4.) The **Hezi Cohen Gallery** can be considered the "free spirit" among the galleries. Hezi Cohen wants to show the artworks in their self-defined nature and provides an exhibition space of 450 m² on two levels that individually adapt to the exhibits. Wolfson St. 54, Tel. 03-639.8788, Mo.-Th. 10.30-19.00, Fr. 10.00-14.00, Sa. 11.00-14.00, info@hezicohengallery.com   , www.hezicohengallery.com

5.) The **Alfred Gallery** was founded in 2005 by a group of artists and is a true non-profit organization. Their aim is to give the not-yet-established a chance to exhibit their work. The exhibits are each of very different kinds (paintings, sculptures, photos, etc.) and are very often rotated with new ones. Simtat Shlush 5, We.-Th. 17.00-21.00, Fr. 10.00-14.00, Sa. 11.00-15.00, Tel. 03-518.3313, http://www.alfredinstitute.org

6.) **Noga Gallery** hosts artworks of prominent as well as promising artists. Most young artists that are supported here are preparing their very first gallery exhibition at all. These young talents ensure the creative and innovative edge of the exhibitions. Mo-Th 11.00-18.00, Fr-Sa 11.00-14.00, Achad Ha'am St 60, tel. 03-566.0123, http://www.nogagallery.com

7.) **Sommer Contemporary Art** was founded in 1999 by Irit Fine Sommer, who has since then not grown weary of searching those artists who have the potential for the big success of tomorrow. Her gallery lifted the local art scene to a new international level. Today her gallery is an institution and is housed in a beautifully renovated building of the early Tel Aviv. Rothschild Blvd. 13, Tel. 3-516.6400, Mo.-Th. 10.00-18.00, Fr. 10.00-14.00, Sa. 11.00-13.00, www.sommergallery.com.

8.) The **Tel Aviv Artists House** belongs to the association of artists and sculptors, a non-commercial organization that takes care of the social needs of artists and dates back to 1934. With its manifold program of activities as well as monthly new exhibitions, this place is an important player in the local art scene. Al-Harizi St. 9, Tel. 03-524.6685, Mo.-Th. 10:00-13:00, 17:00-19:00, Fr. 10:00-13:00, Sa. 11:00-14:00, http://www.artisthouse.co.il, artassoc@012.net.il

9.) Some galleries are a bit more alternative than the others, and their relationship with art is also different, like the **P8 Art Gallery**. They mainly exhibit the works of the five founders, but they also invite others artists to their space. The successful concept has led the group to leave the original space at Poriya St. 8. With the change of location, they aim to establish themselves further on the art market. Ha Patish St. 1, Tel. 050-554.3485, We.-Th. 16.00-20.00, Fr.-Sa. 10.00-14.00, http://www.p8gallery.net, gallery.p8@gmail.com

10.) The **Gallery 21** is a new star among the local galleries. The recent opening was spiced with the participation of several Israeli VIPs, and the public has well noticed this modern and sophisticated venue which specializes in urban and pop-art works. Su-Th 11.00-20.00, Fr 11.00-14.00, Allenby 21, tel 03-903-6339, http://thegallery21.com

11.) **Litvak Gallery** is spectacular on many levels: located on the 23rdf floor with a breathtaking view on Tel Aviv, the gallery exhibits mostly glass art and multimedia works. Equipped with state-of-the-art technology for the perfect sound and the right light, Litvak can truly be called a high-tech gallery. Tel. 03-7163897, Museum Tower, 4 Berkovitz St., 23rd floor, https://www.litvak.com

Theaters and Concert Halls

Tel Aviv has much to offer, even for those who do not speak Hebrew because many performances come with English supertitles, e.g., at the opera. Ballet and contemporary dance are very much worth the visit as well; often these are Israeli productions.

Opera and Theater

1.) Tel Aviv is proud of its opera tradition which dates back to the 1920. Jewish-Russian composer Mordechai Golinkin dedicated his life to the creation of an opera for the Land of Israel. He most probably could have not imagined how much the Israelis would still love opera in the 21st century when he published his thesis, "The Vision of the Hebrew Art Temple of Opera Work in Palestine" in 1917.

Golinkin immigrated in 1923. On 28 July 1923, the "Palestine Opera" was born with the performance of Verdi's "La Traviata." On the way to today's "New Israeli Opera," mainly financial difficulties put the project at risk more than once, but political turbulence also put obstacles along the way. Legend has it that the British Mandate government had asked Golinkin to not show the opera "La Juive" (the Jewess) from HaLevy. The performance had already been very successful in Tel Aviv and was supposed to be shown in Jerusalem, but the British feared problems with the non-Jewish population here: Christians. Golinkin agreed but did not stop the project; he simply changed the title to "Rachel" which was the name of the main figure and performed the opera as scheduled. There are no reports about any negative reactions from the Christians.

Golinkin managed his opera house until 1927 when he left for the US to raise funds. Later, in 1940, George Singer and Riga-born Marc Lavry founded the "Palestine Folk

Opera." Lavry had been the manager of the Berlin Symphony Orchestra between 1929 and 1932, and in the following two years, the opera in Riga. In 1935, he fled to Israel. His opera production "Dan HaShomer" (Dan the Watchman) was shown in Tel Aviv in 1945. It was the first opera production in the country and was based on a play from Shin Shalom. It became Lavry's very own signature to reflect political events in his work, especially topics referring to the European presence in the Near East and the conflicts with the Arab population.

Edis de Philippe (*1912, New York) is another name that is deeply connected with the Israeli opera culture. Singer de Philippe successfully convinced the Zionist Union in Basel that Tel Aviv needed a permanent and locally based opera. From 1947 until her death in 1979, she directed the "National Israeli Opera." Under her auspices, many Israeli but also international singers started their careers, like Plácido Domingo who studied here in the 1960s.

Until 1958, de Philippe was renting space from local theaters and would then move to 1, Allenby Street, the former seat of parliament. In the early years, de Philippe funded the opera house with her own money, but in 1982, it was finally closed due to lack of funding; neither the state nor the municipality was willing to give more grants. De Philippe had been a controversial figure, many would even call her management a dictatorship. She had dedicated her life to the Israeli opera culture and thanks to her, the citizens of Tel Aviv never lost their enthusiasm for it. It is no wonder that in the years following the closure, they would express their displeasure about this loss. Finally, the New Israeli Opera was founded. It is a joint venture between the Cameri Theater and the Israeli Chamber Orchestra which is located in the Tel Aviv Performing Art Center (TAPAC) with 1,500 seats since

1994. The operas are sung in the original language with Hebrew and English supertitles.

Backstage secrets: 90 min before the curtain rises you have the chance to see the artists' final preparations during a half-hour tour. Tickets: 25 NIS, reservation needed: sarah@israelopera.org.il, http://www.israel-opera.co.il (opera -> opera 2018/2019 ->backstage tour) Tel Aviv Performing Arts Center, Sederot Shaul Ha Melech 19, box office: kupa@tapac.org.il, Tel. 03-692.7777,

2.) Every year, more than 900,000 visitors come to the **Cameri Theater** in the TAPAC. Since its founding in 1944, it is an inherent part of Israeli culture. The Cameri wants to give more than a good performance; it wants to bring the theater to everybody. It is a theater with social responsibility: translations into different languages, special tariffs, barrier-free, etc. The Cameri plays with subtitles in English, French, and Russian. Tel Aviv Performing Arts Center, Sederot Shaul Ha Melech. 19, Tel. 03-606.9100, http://www.cameri.co.il

3.) **HaBima** is Israel's national theater. It was founded already in 1913 in Russia and had always struggled with anti-Semitic hostility until the 1920s when the group decided to split during a concert tour in the United States. HaBima started again in 1931 in Tel Aviv and moved into its own theater house in 1945 even before the construction was finished. Since HaBima had been awarded the Israel Prize (that acknowledges engagement for Israeli society) in 1958, the Israelis call it THE Israeli theater house. It is the only member of the European Theater Union (UTE) outside Europe and performs around the globe. Information on performances in English: on request. Kikar HaBima, Tel. 03-629.5555, sherut@habima.org.il, http://www.habima.co.il.

4.) The **Yiddish Theatre** in Israel is one of the most charming among all theaters. As the name already indicates, they play in Yiddish. Headphones with simultaneous translations are provided only in Hebrew and Russian. The company published some examples of its repertoire on YouTube. This way, you can test whether you understand the Yiddish language. The actors are fabulous. They show Jewish culture from many angles, whether traditional, eastern European or modern productions, the Yiddish Theatre hits the mark. The group performs all over the country; in Tel Aviv, they are located at the Tzavta Theater (4a) Ibn Gabirol 30, box office (4b) Carlebach St. 7, , Tel. 03-525.4660, open Su.-Th. 09.00-17.00. http://www.yiddishpiel.co.il

5.) A visit to the **Na Laga'at Center** in Jaffa port is a very enriching experience. While Israeli shops often put little signs on their goods with "na lo laga'at" ("please do not touch,") here, we are in a," please touch" space. Blind and deaf actors present an impressive show with English supertitles. Rezif HaAliya HaShniya, Jaffa Port, Tel. 03-633.0808, http://www.nalagaat.org.il, theater1@nalagaat.org.il, http://www.youtube.com/user/nalagaat

6.) **Mayúmana** is an international creative group that communicates with the audience in its very own way. The participants are actors, musicians, dancers, acrobats in one. Lots of rhythms and visual effects flow from the stage into the audience. Founded by three Israelis, Mayumana has become so successful that they decided to have two groups: one performs in Tel Aviv, and another one is always on tour. Mayúmana House, Yosef Yekutiel 3, Tel. 03-681.1787, http://www.mayumana.com

7.) The **Clipa Theater**, founded in 1995, is considered Israel's best "visual theater." Idit Herman and Dmitry Tyulpanov (†) have founded a company that combines

contemporary dance and musical effects in a new way and
with self-designed costumes. The shows are held either at
a) HaRakevet St. 38 or b) HaRav Kook St 37, tel. 03-
639.9090, info@clipa.co.il, http://www.clipa.co.il

Classical Music

8.) The **Israeli Philharmonic Orchestra (IPO),**
originally "The Palestine Symphony," is world-renowned
and looks back on 75 years of history. On 26 December
1936, the IPO gave its first concert directed by conductor
Arturo Toscanini on the fairgrounds in the north of Tel
Aviv. Prior to this, the Polish violinist Bronisław
Huberman (1882–1947) had convinced 75 Jewish
colleagues from different European countries to
immigrate to Palestine to found a new orchestra.
Huberman saw no future for Jewish musicians in fascist
Europe where more and more of them were harassed and
became jobless. In the first two years, the orchestra would
still play many works from Richard Wagner, a known
anti-Semite, but since the "Night of the Broken Glass"
("Reichskristallnacht") of 9 November 1938, the
orchestra adheres to its ban of Wagner compositions.
1936 was also the year of birth of the Indian conductor
Zubin Mehta who was appointed music director for life of
the orchestra. Since 1968, he had already been their
advisor. Leonard Bernstein (1918-1990) was another big
name that collaborated with the orchestra since 1948, and
who in 1988 became awarded with the title of "conductor
of honor" of the orchestra. Bernstein and Mehta are, of
course, extraordinary musicians, but there is one other
reason why the Israelis love them dearly: both never left
the country during wars. They organized concerts at war
places to morally support the population and the soldiers.
Since 1957, the Frederic R. Mann Auditorium (since 2013
Charles Bronfman Auditorium) at the upper end of
Rothschild Boulevard is the permanent home of the

orchestra, right next to HaBima Theater. The initial building was financially supported by the American philanthropist Frederic R. Mann (1904-1987) from Philadelphia, an international promoter of art and music projects. Charles Bronfman, an American billionaire, supported the last big renovation of the concert hall with $ 7.7 mio under the condition that it would be named after him. Israelis call the venue "heichal ha tarbut," the culture palace. Huberman St. 1, Tel. 03-621.1777, http://www.ipo.co.il

9.) Together with the IPO, the **Israeli Chamber Orchestra (ICO)** belongs to the most renowned in Israel. It was founded in 1965 by Gary Bertini, an Israeli conductor, and composer. The ICO plays music from Israeli and international composers, contemporary as well as baroque. The participation of the ICO at the Wagner festivals in Bayreuth, Germany, in 2011 was discussed very controversially. They were the first Israeli orchestra to play Wagner, unlike the IPO which refused to play Wagner since 1938. Israel Chamber Orchestra, She'erit Israel St. 35, Tickets tel. 03-518.8845-1, http://www.ico.co.il

10.) The youngest of the local orchestras is the **Israeli Contemporary Players (ICP)**. Founded in 1991, the orchestra plays mainly music from the 20th century, often from Israeli composers. The musicians perform at different venues throughout the city; many of their events take place in the Recanati Hall of the Tel Aviv Museum of Art. http://www.ensemble21.org.il

11.) The **Felicja Blumental Music Center** is home to an extensive music library since 1951 and frequently organizes concerts, workshops, and further education. The house is idyllically located next to Tel Aviv's first city hall at the end of Bialik St. In 1991, the center was named after Polish-born pianist Felicja Blumental (1908-

1991.) Since 1999, the Felicja Blumental Festival takes place every year (April/ May), organized from the Tel Aviv Museum of Art. Every day, there are up to 5 events filled with theater plays, music, and films in different venues in the city. Bialik St. 26, Tel. 03-620.1185, info@fbmc.co.il, http://www.fbmc.co.il,

12.) **Tzafta** is a little theater that also offers classical concerts every Saturday at 11.11 am. Ibn Gabirol St. 30, Tel. 03-695.0156/7; opening hours box office: Su.-Th. 10.00-16.00 & 19.00-20.30, Fr: 10.00-14.00 & 19.00-01.00, Sa 10.00-11.30 & 19.00-21.00, www.tzavta.co.il (Hebrew)

13.) The Tel Aviv Museum of Art houses the **Recanati Hall.** Handpicked concert series, contemporary art performances and a high-quality standard turn the hall into a very sought after venue. Shaul Hamelech Blvd. 27, Tel. 03-607.7009, http://www.tamuseum.com/music-lobby, music@tamuseum.com,

Dance

14.) The **Suzanne Dellal Center** is all about dance: education, training, workshops, festivals. Founded in 1989, the center is situated in a palace-like residence in the heart of Neve Tzedek and shows more than 750 events every year. Three stages and the box office are located at the site. Yechieli St. 5, info@sdc.org.il, box office: Tel. 03-510.5656, Opening hours: Su.-Th. 9.00-21.00, Fr. & before holidays: 9.00-13.00, and also 2 hours before the performance starts. http://www.suzannedellal.org.il

Culture - Miscellaneous

Many foreign institutions offer a very interesting cultural program and are very open to tourists and non-Hebrew speakers. Please consult their websites for further information.

15.) **Goethe Institut**, Asia House, Weizmann St. 4, Tel. 03-606.0500, http://www.goethe.de/telaviv (German, Hebrew)

16.) **Instytut Polski**, Beit Psagot, Rothschild Blvd. 3, Tel. 03-696.2053/9, http://www.polishinstitute.org.il (English, Hebrew),

17.) **Czech Centre**, Zeitlin St. 23, Tel. 03-691.1216, http://tel-aviv.czechcentres.cz (Czech, English).

18.) **Romanian Culture Institute**, Shaul Ha Melech 8, Tel. 03-696.1746, http://www.icr.ro/tel-aviv (Romanian, English, Hebrew).

19.) **Instituto Cervantes**, HaArba'a 28 Tel. 03-527.9992, http://telaviv.cervantes.es (Spanish, Hebrew).

20.) **L'Institut Français**, Rothschild Blvd. 7, Tel. 03-796.8000, http://institutfrancais-israel.com/blog/tel-aviv (French, Hebrew)

21.) **Instituto Italiano di Cultura**, HaMered 25, Tel. 03-516.1361, http://www.iictelaviv.esteri.it/IIC_Telaviv (Italian, English, Hebrew), iictelaviv@esteri.it

Tickets

22.) Most of the local event tickets can be purchased at **Le'an** Tel: 03-524.7373 Su-Th 09-19.00, Fr 09.00-13.30, Dizengoff 101

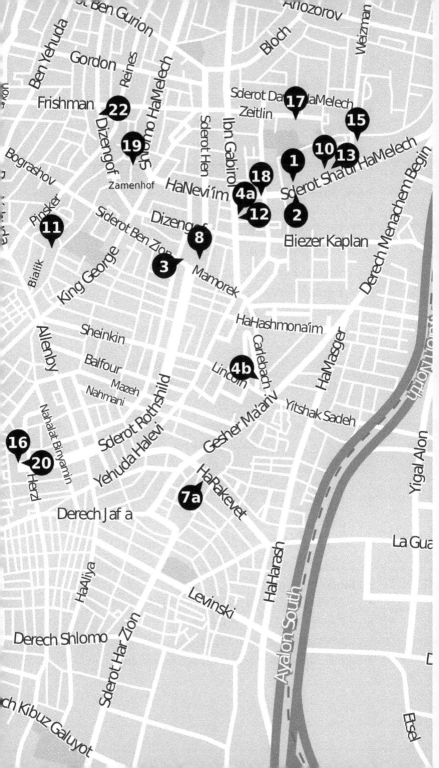

Yearly Events

February
- Marathon Tel Aviv, http://www.tlvmarathon.co.il

March/ April
- Días de Flamenco, http://www.keren-adi.org

May/ June
- Houses from Within, http://www.batim-il.org
- Tel Aviv Pride, https://www.gaytelavivguide.com/
- White Night Festival, https://www.tel-aviv.gov.il
- Student Film Festival, http://www.taufilmfest.com
- Tel Aviv LGBT Film Festival, http://www.tlvfest.com
- Loving Art, Making Art festival (open museums and galleries), www.facebook.com/LovingArt.MakingArt
  - Felicja Blumental International Music Festival http://www.blumentalfestival.com

14-18 May 2019 Eurovision song contest https://eurovision.tv/

July/ August/ September
- Opera in the Park, http://www.israel-opera.co.il
- Madridanza Tel Aviv, http://www.suzannedellal.org.il
- Tel Aviv Dance, http://www.suzannedellal.org.il/
- Houses from Within, http://www.batim-il.org

October/ November
- SPIRIT Film Festival, www.spiritfestival.co.il
- Curtain Up Dance Festival, www.suzannedellal.org.il
- Jaffa Jazz Festival http://eng.hotjazz.co.il/

Israeli Folk Dances For Everybody

The Association of Israeli Folk Dances meets almost every week at Gordon Beach for public dancing. Participation is welcome and free of charge. The dates can be found online: www.harokdim.org/site/markid.htm

Have a shluck and a biss!

Tel Aviv's restaurants are among the most creative and exotic in the world. This special fusion of Jewish traditional food influenced by the immigrants' home countries like Poland, Russia, Morocco, Persia, etc., created a totally new cuisine of "Ethno Food," spiced with the Near East flavor. It is nearly impossible to not eat well in Israel. Even the cocktail bars offer more than just snacks. Every restaurant offers a lunch menu, and in the upper-class restaurants, these are real bargains in comparison to the prices in the evening. The tip is about 15%.

Israelis eat more than they drink and there is practically no bar that does not offer some snacks. Most bars call themselves resto-bars and what they offer is actually more than a simple snack– even at a late hour. While restaurants tend to describe the food on the menu, the street food is for the savvy.

Gastro vocabulary

Sabih

is served in pita bread that is filled with mashed and fried eggplants, sesame cream, a boiled egg, salad, etc., as you like. Ever since sabih was introduced to the local food market by Iraqi Jews, nobody wants to miss it.

Falafel

is also served in pita bread but instead of the eggplant, the falafel contains fried balls from chickpeas and/or fava beans, sesame cream, and pickles as well as tomatoes, onions, etc., add what you like.

Shawarma

comes in different varieties depending on the type of meat and dressing. The thin meat layers are stuffed into the pita bread, and the other ingredients are similar to sabih and falafel, and if you want, you can even add some fries on top.

Laffa

is a large, round, thin bread that is baked on a special curved plate, called Tabun. When finished, it is rolled up together with meat, lettuce, pickles, etc. It is a quite filling meal.

Humus

is made from mashed chickpeas and tahini, lemon juice and olive oil are added as well as garlic and salt. It is served with pita bread. Every Israeli has his/her favorite Hummus shop; in Tel Aviv, most are located in the south.

Shakshuka

is a pan dish mixing fresh tomatoes, herbs, onions, sometimes also chili before eggs are finally added. Originally from Northern Africa, Shakshuka has become the Israeli national dish. Most hotels have it on their buffet.

Jachnun

is a gift of the Yemeni cuisine. The thin sweet sheets of dough are rolled up and cooked for 10 hours. They are eaten with an egg and hot sauce.

Where to eat?

Of course, this depends. The longer you live in Tel Aviv, the more you will become an expert yourself. The following places attract a large audience with what they have to offer:

Sabih and Falafel

1.) **Shlomo & Sons** have been located directly on the green center strip of Sderot Nordau / corner Ben Yehuda for over 40 years. It is one of the best falafel places in town. They also make fresh salads, omelets, and Shakshuka.

2.) **Sabih Frishman**. You cannot miss it: right on the corner of Frishman and Dizengoff Street, you will see a long line of people waiting for their food.

Humus

Everybody claims to know the best Hummus place. The traditional shops open in the morning, and once the fresh Hummus is sold, they close again, normally in the early evening, or even before.

3.) **Abu Hassan** (Ajami) is a classic. Abu Hassan has been around for ages and can be considered a landmark. The place opens at 8.00 in the morning and by 15.00 is already closed again, all the hummus is sold. You can dine in or take it home. 1, HaDolfin St. Ajami, border with Jaffa.

4.) **Abu Dubby** (center-north) offers Hummus with Jamaica flavor. You may enjoy your hummus together with reggae music, even on Shabbat. 81, King George St. 81/ Bar Giora.

Shakshuka

You will find it on nearly every menu, and in your hotel buffet even in the morning. But one restaurant you must not miss:

5.) "**Dr. Shakshuka**" is for sure the uncrowned shakshuka king from Tripoli (3, Beit Eshel St. near Clock Tower). This place also opens already in the morning. The plates are generous and filling. If you are not very hungry in the morning, you might consider sharing a course.

The more home-made variants, as they are eaten in many Israeli homes every day, offer smaller and more economic portions. A good example is Shlomo & Sons (1).

Is all that kosher?

Tel Aviv is a very secular city, and not all restaurants are kosher (in Hebrew: ka-shér, meaning: suitable), but many are. If you are still wondering why there is no cheese on the salami pizza or why that cheese is artificial, here is a little introduction to the Jewish dietary laws, called kashrut (speak: kash-root)

What is kashrut?

Kashrut is a dietary law. It prescribes which foods may be eaten at all, especially which animals (see 3rd book of Moses.) It is not allowed to consume blood, and meat and dairy have to be strictly separated from each other (no cheeseburger, no cordon bleu allowed.) Neutral foods are "párveh," meaning "not dairy," not meat, e.g., vegetables and fruits. Cheese is a difficult product since it is made with the help of lab-ferment, traditionally coming from animals, but nowadays it is possible to make hard cheese from microbial lab-ferment.

How do I know whether it is kosher?

Kosher food is labeled, and so are the restaurants. The label can also be found on products that are naturally kosher like wine, but where the production in an un-kosher factory could add impurities. The label is supervised by the rabbinate. In the US, you often find on the products the letter "U" from the Orthodox Union. In other countries, it might look like a stamp and shows the name of the certifier.

Coffee & Cafés

Israelis love coffee and dispute with Spaniards and Italians who makes the best. The big Israeli coffee shop chain AROMA CAFÉ (black logo, white and red letters) offers not only hot drinks and cakes but also salads and sandwiches. At the port (nemal) of Tel Aviv, you will find a couple of cafés next to the water where you can sit down on the big wooden step and enjoy a coffee or while contemplating the sea.

Do you drink your coffee with milk? You might want to try an "upside-down coffee," called coffee afuch, where the milk sits on top of the coffee. In summer, you will find many cafés offering "coffee barad," in Europe called frappé, with crushed ice. The Israelis have a product even for the lovers of Turkish coffee: the "mud coffee," coffee botz. Turkish coffee is put together with sugar into the cup and hot water added.

6.) Founded in 1919 by **Moshe Landwer** from Berlin, Landwer was Israel's first coffee brand. The Café Landwer is an old classic in Tel Aviv. It has become a chain with several venues in the city. One of the nicest can be found in the Gan Meir Park (Rabenu Tam St. 7) This little oasis seems to be far away from the buzzing city and invites you to stay for a coffee and some cake or sandwich, or soup, or… . Other nice Landwer Cafés are the ones at the marina (Yordei HaSira 2) and in the shopping village of Sarona. Generally, Landwer is open daily from 08.00-00.00. www.landwercafe.co.il/

7.) **Dallal** is not only an exquisite restaurant, but they also have an excellent bakery-café close by (Kol Israel Haverim 7) Mousses, éclairs, tarts, quiches… the most exquisite pastries lie at your feet. A great place to have a coffee in the center of Neve Tzedek.Su.-Th. 07.00-20.30, Fr. 07.00-17.00, http://dallal.co.il

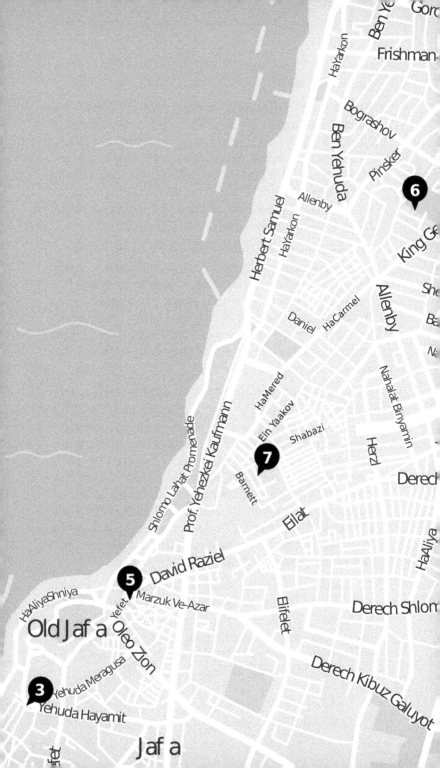

8.) **Max Brenner** (45, Rothschild Blvd., more branches on the website) is the name of Tel Aviv's chocolate planet. Chocolate in all varieties (to eat, to drink, hot, cold, spiced, black, white…) can be found on the menu and in the shop. Max Brenner also functions as a bistro and offers a creative selection of sandwiches, pasta, entrecotes, and salads. Opens daily at 09.00 am. http://www.maxbrenner.com

Restaurants

The Israeli dress code is rather casual, but always cool. This is important. Nobody will turn you away only because you are wearing jeans or the wrong label. Even outdoor sandals are not a general no-go, but: the better the restaurant, the less people are willing to see outdoor fashion.

Even though you can pay with credit card in nearly all places, little neighborhood eateries will not likely accept them. Here are some recommendations to have the ultimate local gourmet experience:

Yemenite

The following selected Yemenite restaurants are little family eateries around the Carmel Market where the neighborhood has lunch at reasonable prices. In the little streets around the market, you will discover even more. The tasty food is served with bread and spicy sauces (skhug). Having lunch here will make you feel like a local. Between 12.00 and 13.30, the places are very full and you might have to wait a bit for a table.

1.) **Eres**. Great quality for little money. Probably one of the best shnitzels in town. Nahliel St. 24, Tel. 03-510.2555

2.) **Rina & Zacharia**. Their soups are legendary, and the house specializes in typical Yemenite food with a variety of meat. HaKovshim St. 22

Oriental

3.) **Mi-ve-Mi** is an institution in Tel Aviv. For decades this family-run eatery prepares freshly grilled meat with typical local side dishes. Prices are rather moderate for that quality. Their home-made desert "Bavarian crème" is something you will never get at any of the other places. Open every day, all day from 09.30-22.45. Derech Menachem Begin 35, tel. 3-560-1325

4.) **Maganda** is a small kosher restaurant with a very long tradition. The quality of their meat is worth every shekel! It is located at the same place since its founding back in 1927. The restaurant is richly decorated with historic photos and newspaper clippings. The kitchen is a journey through the Middle East. They also offer excellent wines from the Golan Heights. Rabbi Meir St. 26, Tel. 03-517-9990, http://www.maganda.co.il/

Fusion/ Mediterranean

The Jewish immigration from different countries has left its mark on the local cuisine and over the years, the chefs have created dishes nobody wants to miss.

5.) **Claro** belongs to the famous Israeli chef Ran Shmueli and is a new star on Tel Aviv's gourmet sky. Houses in a historic Templer building, the restaurant offers mediterranean kitchen with Israeli flavor. Rav Aluf David Elazar St. 30, Tel. 3-6017.777. http://www.clarotlv.com/

6.) **Cheder Ha Ochel / The Dining Hall** and is located at the Tel Aviv Performing Art Center (TAPAC.) Have a seat at the long tables and enjoy the company. The restaurant presents itself in a very modest style and focuses on the food which comes like tapas in little portions. Due to its proximity to the opera, this place is very full shortly before and after the performance. Shaul Ha Melech Blvd. 23, Tel. 03-696.6188.

7.) The name **Coffee Bar** is a discreet understatement for a restaurant in the budgetary upper middle class. Located since 1994 in an area where not many go for a stroll, the Coffee Bar has become one of the best restaurants in town. It is open 7 days a week; breakfast is served from 09.00-12.00, except on Shabbat when a special family lunch is offered. From Sunday to Thursday, they offer a business lunch from 12.00-17.00, the dinner follows on seamlessly, Haruzim St. 13, Tel. 03-688.9696, http://www.coffeebar.co.il

Outside

8.) Neve Tzedek without **Susanna**? Impossible! In the heart of Neve Tzedek, a beautiful terrace offers a shady refuge on those hot days. Whether you are simply looking for a nice cup of good coffee or a large dinner, Susanna's kitchen is delicious and also suitable for vegetarians! In summer they open the roof terrace. With a drink in your hand, you can now enjoy the village flair of this beautiful old neighborhood. Shabazi St. 8, Tel. 03-517.7580.

9.) Das **Bellini** is located close to the Suzanne Dellal Center. A nice Italian family restaurant on a quiet side street with a shady terrace. Open every day from 12.00 to midnight, the Bellini offers a very good menu with renowned Italian food and dishes from "la mamma." Every day, there is a different lunch special, or you can eat à la carte. Yechieli St. 6, Tel. 057-943.619, http://www.bellini.co.il.

10.) **Vicky Cristina** is a tapas bar and restaurant in the old train station HaTachana. The wine bar curls around the big old tree and the guests enjoy Spanish rhythm, beautiful decor, food (from Vicky) and wine (from

Cristina) as if they were in Spain. Wine is their specialty; the list contains 120 different names. Tel. 03-736.7272, http://www.vicky-cristina.co.il/

Jewish / Eastern European

11.) **Tash and Tasha** is the Georgian experience in an Israeli environment. Modern Georgian cuisine presented in a cozy location in Jaffa by an enthusiastic and welcoming staff, what else can you wish for? If you want to be on the safe side: make a reservation, the place is popular. Beit Eshel St. 31, tel. 03-677-1373, Su-Th 17.00-00.00, Fr-Sa 12.00-00.00.

12.) **Little Prague**, is more a pub than a restaurant but also offers typical Czech food like goulash, schnitzel, cake with lemon icing, etc., and, of course, many Czech beers. Allenby St. 56, Tel. 03- 516.8137., http://www.littleprague.co.il/

13.) **Keton** opened in the 1940s and legend has it that the menu is still the same: kugel (sweet noodle gratins), fish, soups..., well-proven typical East-European, Jewish cuisine. Dizengoff St. 145, Tel. 03-523.3679, https://www.keton.co.il/

Vegetarian/ Vegan

14.) **Nanuchka** is a legendary Georgian restaurant with a special flair: nice furniture, fresh flowers and old porcelain with flower design. The guests quickly feel at home and at the end of the evening, most have made new friends or dance on the bar. The later the hour, the better the party. The kitchen is very creative: when local ingredients meet Georgian tradition, the result is amazing. In 2014, the restaurant decided to become vegan. Tel. 03-516.2254, Lilienblum St. 30 http://nanuchka.co.il/

15.) **Meshek Barzilay** is proof that vegan food is already playing in the gourmet league. In this restaurant you will

not only find healthy, seasonal food that tickles all your taste buds, butyou will also have a hard time taking your eyes off the beautiful food design. The place is open all day from 08.00-23.00 (opens Sundays at 09.00). Their power-breakfast sets the tone for an energetic day. Achad Ha'am 6, Tel. 03-516.6329, http://www.meshekbarzilay.co.il/

Gluten-free

16.) **HaKosem** is one of the very few places in town that offer gluten-free falafel with gluten-free pita. While you stand in line, chances are the lovely staff will offer you some samples. Opens already 09.30 in the morning. Shlomo Ha Melech St. 1, Tel. 03-525-2033, http://www.falafelhakosem.com/

Meat

Most Tel Aviv restaurants offer a very good meat quality, but some of them should not be missed by carnivores (see also no. 3 and 4):

17.) Nomen est omen, **Makom Shel Basar** means "Place of Meat," and here they demand a great deal of their own meat production. The restaurant has its own rooms and equipment for meat hanging and additional processing. The excellent wine selection makes the menu perfect. Makom Shel Basar is located close to Rothschild Blvd. where Neve Tzedek starts. Guests can also enjoy their meal on a very nice terrace. Meat dishes start at 130 NIS. Shabazi St. 64, Tel. 03-510.4021

18.) **Rak Basar** – "Only Meat" is the motto of this meat restaurant and this is the understatement of the century! Eating at Rak Basar is a great experience. Like in a butcher's shop, the guest can choose the piece with the help from an expert. Like in Makom Shel Basar, the meat is produced in-house and sold by weight. Derech Shlomo 19, Tel. 01700-550.028.

Fish/ Seafood

19.) **Manta Ray** is the restaurant with the "killer location" as critics call it: Alma Beach between Charles Clore Park and Etzel Museum. The prices are still very reasonable for such an excellent oriental restaurant (main dishes start at 90 NIS.) The Manta Ray considers itself a fish restaurant, but they also serve good entrecote and even vegetarian dishes. Every day from 09.00 to 12.00, the Manta Ray serves a wonderful breakfast with pancakes, omelet, fruit, champagne… and the beach! In the afternoons, you can enjoy the beach and later, the sunset with coffee and an amazing dessert (e.g., caramelized figs) and a good drink. Tel. 03-517.4773, mail@mantaray.co.il, http://www.mantaray.co.il

Exquisite

20.) **Messa** is the stylish restaurant of chef Aviv Moshe. His specialty is the Nouvelle French Cuisine with creations like a caramelized fish with tempura avocado and lychee jelly. You need to reserve your table 2 days in advance! Open daily from 12.00-15.30 and 19.00-24.00. HaArba'a St. 19, Tel. 03-685.6859, messa@messa.co.il, http://messa.rest.co.il/

21.) **Dallal** travels back with you into the time when Neve Tzedek was a place for Jewish entrepreneurs who had decided to leave the then-claustrophobic and crowded Jaffa to build their new homes here. This romantic restaurant was built on the ruins of three old houses, with an intimate courtyard and open-air bar. The menu is well balanced between fish and meat dishes and an additional dish of the day. Shabazi St. 10, Tel. 03-510.9292. dallal@dallal.info, http://www.dallal.info

Breakfast

Israelis appreciate a good breakfast and nearly all restaurants start the day latest at 09.00 with a breakfast menu, whether it is the Manta Ray or the Café Landwer, they are all prepared for hungry early morning guests. The restaurant Dellal has even its own bakery and café, but the most renowned place for breakfast is Benedict.

22.) **Benedict** – "All about breakfast" (29, Rothschild Blvd.), their slogan says it all, and every child in Tel Aviv knows Benedict. Benedict serves breakfast 24/7: pancakes, champagne, orange juice, croissants, eggs … the perfect start into the day! More branches are listed on their website. Tel. 03-686.8657, http://www.benedict.co.il

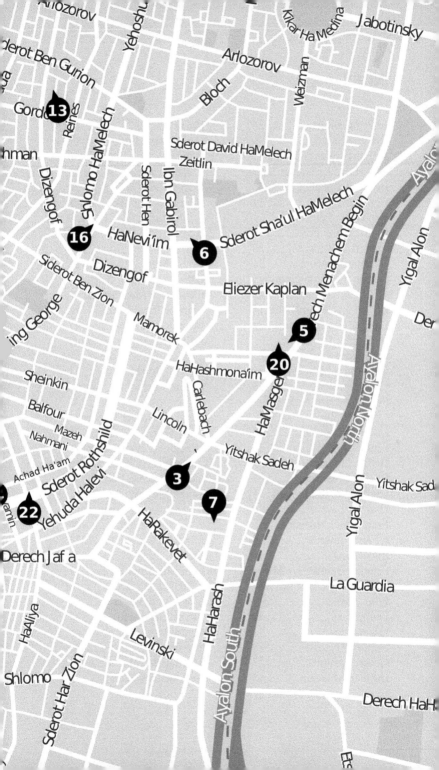

INDEX

Lightning Source UK Ltd.
Milton Keynes UK
UKHW031639280519
343449UK00037B/576/P